How to get your shit together!

A semi spiritual guide to a happy life.

To my loving partner Brian

To my amazing sons Kai, Hagen and Erik

To my partner in crime and wonderful soul mate, Ulli.

I love you

Bibliographical information of the German National Library. The German National Library registers this publication in the German National Bibliography. Detailed data can be obtained at http://dnb.dnb.de.

© 2018 Judy Berens
www.takodavillage.com
takoda@takodavillage.com
Printed and published by:
BoD – Books on Demand, Norderstedt

ISBN: 9783748132929

Content

Prologue

My name is Judy; I am now 44 years old; and I believe in changing the world. How? By helping people find their own personal happy, because many happy people add up to a happy world.

First, let me tell you a little about myself. I was a happy child with a disposition for depression. Of course, no one knew that at the time. Born shortly after the second World War in Germany, my parents grew up with very little money, very little food and very little time for love and affection. My father met his father when he was five years old in 1947, after he returned from two years of Russian imprisonment. My grandfather was very strict and abusive which, of course, led to a rather troubled childhood for my father. Compared to my granddad, my father was great. Compared to other dads, he was very strict, high tempered, unpredictable, and never refused to give a good old spanking. He was also career-oriented, making a lot of money and granting my brother and me almost every wish possible. As you can see, for me growing up, this was quite a roller coaster and way too much to have to deal with as a child.

When I was sixteen years old, my dark phase began. I loved sad poetry, dark music and anything dramatic. I had dyed my hair black and spent my time obsessed with death, hoping to be rescued by someone handsome who would understand and love every part of me. During really hard times, I cut my arm with an old, dull razor. Not very deep at all, just enough to see a little blood. It helped release some of the unexplainable pain and pressure I felt inside. On top of all of that, I was not interested in anything really, except for hanging out with my best friend. I did not understand the world; my grades were average or below; and it was just not possible to motivate me for anything. Looking back, I am often surprised about how things always just seemed to work out for me even though I did nothing for it. I guess the universe played a very important part in leading me in certain directions.

Eventually I snapped out of it. It was a rational decision, actually. I decided to grow up, changed everything about myself and fell in love with a student of law. I dressed up pretty; my hair was almost blond; I stopped painting dark and gloomy pictures; and I pretended to be happy. No, I actually believed I was happy.

My husband was not a very nice man. I wasn't able to find a nice man, because when you are broken on the inside, you don't get what you want; you get what you need. And I needed to learn. But did I understand? No. How could I? I had no knowledge of life and having been raised by a very stern father who would not accept any kind of talk back what so ever, I believed it to be normal to be bossed around and humiliated. I never stood up for myself because I always believed I was wrong. I didn't want to be overly sensitive or a problem for anyone. I just wanted to be loved, and I did everything I could to make my husband love me. But he didn't. He was an absolute narcissist, not capable of loving anyone but himself, and I was so far away from the person I was meant to be, that I wasn't even able to love myself. And still, we had three wonderful children together. Then, when our youngest was only 9 months old, I had my first mental breakdown. At first, I did not realize what it was because it felt just like a horrible stomach flu. Only I could not vomit. I simply felt incredibly sick physically and absolutely terrified and hopeless mentally. My world had turned black from one second to the next, and I was completely lost. The medication I received started working after about three weeks, and I was capable of taking care of things again. Not the way I functioned before the breakdown, though. Before, I had a part time job, took care of the kids and the apartment and supported my husband with his own business. After the breakdown, I did not feel capable of working next to all the other things I had on my plate. Having to go back to work simply terrified me because I still suffered from anxiety. My husband, on the other hand, was not capable of supporting the family by himself, although he never really admitted it. Me not working made him angry which lead to him treating me even worse. Of course, I let it happen. I gave him the freedom to treat me the way he did. I did not defend myself, nor did I set any boundaries. At first. After many hours of talking to my dearest friend, I realized something was very wrong. But it was too late. So many things had happened that there was no fixing this relationship. After one year of struggle, I left my husband.

My life started to change when I read the book: "Ich Stehe Nicht Mehr Zur Verfügung" by Olaf Jacobsen. It is a German book, and roughly translated it would be called "I am no longer available." Although the book mostly talked about the roles people play and the energies one can absorb without knowing it, it opened the door for me to a whole new spiritual world. You see, I was always a believer, yet I was never religious. I just cannot identify with any of the religions I got to know. But I always knew, there is more than meets the eye and we don't come out of nowhere. The book which then ultimately changed my life is called: "Quanten Herz" (quantal heart) by Céline Kever. The book explains the seven hermetic universal principles and offers exercises and tools to change your life. For me, this book made so much sense. I finally understood what life is all about, where we come from and why, and how important it is to take personal responsibility for your life and your happiness.

I did have another breakdown. Thankfully, it was not as bad as the first one. I do have to take medication, because my new psychiatrist explained to me that my condition is inherited. It is caused by a hormonal imbalance, and the medication I receive treats just that which leads to me being capable and awake and enthusiastic about life and love and everything beautiful.

My journey up until now was a long and very difficult one, even if it may not appear so in this rather short summary. I had many, very hard life lessons to endure until I finally found myself and recognized my own self-worth. I have received many chances and opportunities, and the more I learned, the more support I received and the easier it got. After my first breakdown and leaving my husband, I had no job, no supporting family, a rundown apartment and no hope. Now I have a new partner, and we live in a wonderful house with the kids, three cats and four guinea pigs. We own two horses and have jobs and a wonderful circle of friends. I am not where I want to be just yet, but I am very happy where I am.

I sincerely hope that this book will help you go to wherever you wish to be.

The Hermetic Philosophy of Ancient Egypt and Greece – The Kybalion

Intro

The Kybalion is a book written by three authors who do not want to be named; therefore they refer to themselves as the three initiates. It explains the seven hermetic principles. You know, the ones that completely changed my life. The legend says that Hermes Trismegistos, a messenger of the gods, was sent to earth in order to induct certain people into the universal laws composed of the seven hermetic principles. Hermes did so for many years and his students did so for many years as well, yet nothing was ever written down. Only very few people received the privilege of this knowledge until we reached the early nineteen hundreds, when these three initiates believed the time had come to present this philosophy to the many in the form of a book. I suppose they knew the world was ready. Especially since knowledge of that sort only reaches the ones whose minds are prepared for it.

I will now get into these seven principles. The Principle of Mentalism explains where everyone and everything comes from. A source of loving energy, many of us refer to as god. The Principle of Correspondence teaches us how your outside world corresponds to your inside world and that your thoughts manifest themselves in reality. The Principle of Vibration talks about the oscillation of energy and how this effects our reality as well. The Principle of Polarity and The Principle of Rhythm explain our part and our responsibility in transforming our live by staying positive and choosing to not let circumstances drag us down. The Principle of Cause and Effect helps us understand predestination and the possibility to live a self-determined live within this principle. The Principle of Gender teaches us about the two necessary energies, male and female, that are basic elements of everything. Please know the hermetic philosophy is far more than what I will explain. This book is meant as a guide, the principles as a foundation. If you wish to learn more about this philosophy, there is plenty of literature available.

It does help immensely if you are a somewhat spiritual person. But if you are not, please bear with me. I am convinced this book can help you to a certain, but very important, extent as well.

The Principle of Mentalism

The principle of mentalism states that everything is energy, because energy is the source of everything. The only difference between all there is, is the frequency of oscillation. The universe, the creation, god, the divine or simply the one is pure energy with an oscillation of very high frequency. I like to refer to it as the source, because it is what created everything else. The source created us and parts of it are always within each and every one of us; a divine core or our soul, if you wish. This divine core connects us to everything, especially each other. If I hurt someone, I, therefore, hurt myself as well, for we both are connected through our soul. The other persons divine core is also my divine core. All of us come from the source and all of us will return to it because all of us belong together. I prefer the term "source", because it is not as cliché as the term "universe" and it is not as controversial as the term "god" may be. Yet all these terms are of course valid, for they all come down to the same thing, namely divine creation of life.

With this in mind, it makes sense that people are able to create a collective consciousness. If more and more people have the same insight, the faster it will spread. Just think of fashion trends, for instance. Imagine what we could turn this world into if all of us had loving and kind thoughts at all times.

The principle of mentalism is very hard to grasp. This is where you simply believe. The human mind is quite capable, but the source is so complex, that it by far exceeds the boundaries of our understanding. Have faith in where you come from and know that everyone is beautiful and of indescribable worth.

The source does not judge. The source is unconditional and everlasting, pure love. It is the only constant in the entire universe. And it is part of you. It is deep within you and it will guide you, if you only let it.

ಏ ● ಐ

When I was a young girl I had anxiety attacks. I never told anyone about them because they would overcome me at night, when I went to bed, and I did not know what they were. All I knew was how I felt, which was quite terrible. I experienced incredible fear of life, to the point where I felt nauseous and alone and hopeless. I was a catholic girl and believed in god. So one night, when the attack hit me very hard, I folded my hands, closed my eyes and began praying. "Please, dear god. Make it go way. Make it never come back. Please dear god, I beg you, make it go away..." I did this for a few minutes when suddenly the feeling disappeared. It did not disappear forever, but at least for the rest of my childhood.

I did lose faith in the catholic religion with time, simply because I could not identify with it, although I still have many friends that do. However, I never lost faith in that higher power that rescued me back when I was only 9 years old. No matter how much I doubted things, and no matter how much I wondered what really is out there, I always knew it was something loving and wonderful. I simply had to find a way to connect.

Now, having found that lost connection. I never feel alone and scared, because deep inside I feel the presence and the love and the support of the divine.

The Principle of Correspondence

Energy vibrates. Since all is energy, everything vibrates. Sensitive people are aware of that because they can feel it, even though a lot of times they may not know what it is they are feeling. For a better understanding, the hermetic philosophy describes a model of three energetic planes.

- The great material plane
- The great intellectual plane
- The great spiritual plane

This is, of course, very simplified. Between the planes is a smooth transition but know, as the frequency of the material plane is rather low, the frequency of the spiritual plane is very high and the closest to the source. All of the principles apply to all of the planes.

Because of the low frequency of the material plane, it contains everything that is part of the material world. Bodies of all kinds, liquids, gases, heat, light, simply everything we can place into our physical universe. We are part of this plane because of our physical body.

The great intellectual plane can be understood as a bridge between the material and the spiritual plane.

Its frequency is much higher, and it is trainable. The more spiritual you are, the easier it will be for you to access this plane. Depending on your focus, your attention and your affection it can increase its frequency within and around you, helping you to develop helpful and healing skills. We are part of this plane, because of our mind and our capability to think about and understand things. This plane is the key to our intellectual elevation.

The great spiritual plane is the one closest to god. Its frequency is immense and in order to reach it, we have to be able to do the following.

- Sense ourselves
- Be aware of our divine core
- Realize with all of our heart how we are all connected with each other and are therefore one

It is not enough to know and believe these facts in order to reach the spiritual plane. You have to be convinced, feel and understand it. It is a way of life. This may take a little practice, but eventually it will all make sense. Trust me.

Humans are able to reach all three planes because we are physical, mental and spiritual beings. I do believe animals are no different than us when it comes to accessing these planes, with the exception that most animals surely do not have to train themselves to reach the spiritual plane.

It is also important to understand how the world and the life you live is a mirror. Anything and everything that goes on within you will be reflected. This way, you are actually always able to know if your body, mind and soul are healthy. Is your life chaotic? Do you get into fights a lot? Are you frustrated, do bad things happen to you or do you always meet the "wrong" people who don't treat you the way you wish to be treated?

Or, do you feel blessed, balanced and grateful? Do you keep your cool, stay positive, and look for solutions? Are you surrounded by wonderful people and love?

It is our thoughts that create our reality! Our thoughts are energy as well, and they are so much more powerful than most people believe. If doubts and fears are on your mind, then you will attract situations that make you doubt and fear. We always attract what we are focused on because energy always follows the attention. Your mind is basically a magnet, attracting whatever goes on inside of you.

Your mind is the creator of all that is around and within you.

Everything equates to something. You can always see the great within the tiny, and the tiny within the great. Remember your life is a mirror of what is going on within you. It equates to your state of mind. If you change how you think and feel, the entire world around you will change as well. How your life develops lies in your direct responsibility. This I cannot emphasize enough.

⁝ ● ⁞

When I was ill with depression and anxiety, I was not able to focus on anything. I was always afraid of what gave me the anxiety, and I was afraid of never getting well and always having to feel this incredible and unbearable pain. I missed appointments; I was overwhelmed with the simplest tasks; and every single day seemed to be an exhausting battle. All of this chaos on the inside led to chaos on the outside. I was not able to keep a clean and organized home; I felt overwhelmed with work; I was weak and insecure, as I could not even order a pizza by myself. Since I was always scared of being alone, my husband left me alone all the time because he was reacting to the energy I was sending. And feeling like a victim, automatically turned me into a victim, because I allowed him to treat me like one. My thoughts and fears created my reality. Life was very hard back then. However, the more order I created within me, the more order was created around me. Eventually I was in control again. Eventually I recognized the mirrors in my environment and used them to transform myself. As I transformed on the inside, my environment transformed on the outside as well.

The Principle of Vibration

As mentioned before, everything is always in vibration, and the higher the frequency, the closer it is to pure and loving spiritual energy.

Our oscillation is an interface to the outside world. We constantly send and receive our and other energies, yet we can only receive energy of the same frequency as what we are sending. If your thoughts are unkind or fearful, doubtful and frustrated, then that is exactly the energy you are sending into the world which leads to you receiving nothing but situations equating to fear, doubt and frustration. Obviously this principle is closely connected to the principle of correspondence as they both create mirrors of your life. Look within you and find what really is there. If you are caught within a negative spiral, this is where to begin the transformation into an upward and positive spiral.

Most people are not aware of their thoughts. They do not realize how many thoughts are unhealthy, slowing down their own oscillation. It is of utmost importance to be aware of your thoughts. This is something that truly does need to be trained if you wish to change your life into a happier and more fulfilling one. Your attitude towards life creates your life. Slow moving energy causes illness and unhappiness. Only fast moving energy gets you where you need to be, namely in a place of balance and fulfillment.

Do not judge, have faith, be humble, grateful, helpful, kind and free of prejudice and you will receive vibrations of very high frequency. Your life will change into a very happy and positive one, because the faster our energy vibrates, the closer we are to the pure, divine energy of the source.

Please know that everything happens for a reason, and there will always be new possibilities to reach your highest potential.

ℴ●ℭ

I try to watch my thoughts all the time. I think carefully about whatever I am about to say, before I say it. And still, negative words and thoughts happen. But, they happen much less. When I first started working on this, I merely forbade myself to think or say mean things. This does not mean I never think or speak my truth. I do believe there are bad people in this world and saying how I feel, when I am asked, is perfectly all right. I do not dwell on it, however, and I try not to judge.

As I got more and more practice, I slowly started to feel a difference as well. When I get caught up in a negative situation, not realizing it, I complain and worry, forget all the good until I start feeling bad. I actually feel my energy frequency slowing down, making me weak and tired. Realizing this, I can counteract and as soon as I focus on the positive things in my life. My energy speeds up again, which is a great support to solving the problem that has been on my mind before.

A colleague at work, whom I used to be friends with, had the tendency to speak ill of almost everyone. I had the tendency to go along with it thinking we were not speaking ill at all; we were simply speaking the truth. But who were we to judge what other people are like or how they should be? We had no right and no ability to do so. After a few months, I started realizing that the way I was speaking about people and the judgements I made without knowing anything about them was making me feel bad. No matter how much you justify yourself, your divine core will let you know that what you are doing is not healthy for you or for anyone else. As I stopped engaging in these conversations, I started feeling better, even when my friend distanced herself from *me (which was very painful at first, but also very necessary). It was one of those lessons where you need to learn to let go.*

The Principle of Polarity

We live in a world of duality composed of opposites. Trust and fear are opposites. They are two poles of the same thing, the same emotion. Heat and cold are also two opposites of the same thing – temperature. It is very important to realize something is hot or cold, without judging if that is a good or a bad thing. Your freezing might be somebody else's refreshment. Judging others or yourself does not help. On the contrary, it just slows down your energy. If there is something that needs to be changed or taken care of, do it. Don't judge yourself by getting angry for making a mistake or for having unhealthy habits or for being stuck in a traffic jam. And don't judge others as well, for everyone walks on their own path at their own pace, with their own problems and lessons and obstacles. Help, don't judge. Criticize if you must, but don't judge. Be honest and loving to yourself and others; set boundaries and do what is necessary to protect your life and your loved ones; but don't judge. It's a waste of time and energy!

As I have mentioned before, everything happens for a reason. So if we first accept things as they are, we should then ask ourselves the following:

- What is the universe trying to tell me?
- What inside of me has attracted this situation?
- Which topic is being dealt with?

It is not always easy to find the answers to these questions, but finding them leads to hermetic alchemy and therefore freedom. Conversations with friends and loved ones can be helpful. Try to be honest with yourself; name the things as they are; and remember not to judge. Not everything that is being presented to you is something you will like. That's perfectly okay, but ignoring it will not get you one step further. It needs to come out and be taken care of, for only the answers to those questions can help transform your life. Or maybe not, depending how wonderful your life already is, as it can be quite refreshing to answer these questions in very positive situations as well.

The opposites are not only in their being oppositional, but in their oscillation as well. Take love and hate for instance. Both are an emotion, and if you imagine a scale, hate could be around -20 whereas love would be +20. This is just an example, for you cannot really measure emotions like that. Anyway, the pole with the higher oscillation is always the dominant one and therefore the one closest to the source. It's the one that feels right and good because it is supported by the source. In this case, love. Fear and hate do not feel good. Neither does anger. But love and trust do, as does understanding. Don't get me wrong though, you should never not defend yourself for the sake of not getting angry. Protecting your core is part of your self-worth and although it does not feel good to carry out conflicts of any sort, sometimes it just cannot be avoided.

So even if there will always be unpleasant situations, keep your focus on the positive things in your life. Concentrate on all the presents you have received, not the problems. By presents I mean everything good you might have like a roof over your head, health, a job, a pet, your favorite shampoo and whatever else might make your day. Of course, problems need to be taken care of, but do not dwell on them. Think about all the good and remain in a place of high oscillation.

This is easy when everything is all right. But what if it isn't? Don't be too hard on yourself if you cannot keep your energy level high at all times. We are only human, and it is natural. But you can keep it from dropping all the way down by doing the following:

- **Be grateful** for everything you have achieved, even the little things. You can make it a little ritual to give thanks for ten different reasons, every morning you get ready. Be grateful for finding your favorite shampoo at the store, for your best friend, for the sunny day, for a delicious lunch and anything else you enjoy. Being aware of everything good, even if it seem very insignificant, will change your energy level and help you focus on the dominant poles.

- **Meditate** in whatever way you can. I, for instance, usually meditate while taking a bath or cleaning the house, because I am doing something I don't really have to concentrate on, so my mind goes flying and very often I receive many, helpful insights I was not able to think of before. When it comes to a specific subject I want to meditate over, I sometimes do it the classical way. I sit down comfortably, close my eyes, focus on the subject and wait for whatever will turn up in my mind.

- **Think positive**. Within every situation lies a present. Something to learn, something to gain. Many situations are not even negative at all, we just think they are. We think a person finds us annoying because we caught them looking at us funny. What we don't know is that the person was not really looking at us at all. The person was lost in thought and happened to make a weird face. Too fast we tend to think and expect the worst, believing it will save us disappointment. But guess what, even if you expect the worst und your worries actually come true, you will still be disappointed and you will have spent a lot of time expecting bad things. If you only expect and believe good things, you might still get disappointed every once in a while, but most of the time you will simply be happy because you feel and see the good in everything. Furthermore, as we have learned through the principle of correspondence, you receive what you send, so that's another plus.

- **Remember your dreams and goals** and see yourself achieving them. Visualize yourself driving that awesome car and earning all that money. See yourself owning a little coffee shop or writing a book or getting that job or feeling fulfilled and happy. Do not put a "someday" in those dreams. Pretend the car is already parked in your garage and look through catalogues to pick out furniture for your customers. Turn up your frequency, focus your energy and materialize your dreams and goals.

- **Be aware** that both poles are always connected to each other. The opposite one is therefore always reachable, as presented in the graphic above. It is up to you which end you chose.

During my three single years after I had left my husband, I met a handful of men I thought could be my new partner, but none of them were. I tried not to be pushy, to stay impartial and remain patient, and I really believed I was. But the men I met seemed to be playing with me, leading me on, making me believe they wanted a serious relationship; however, when we got to that point, all of them skipped out.

What was the universe trying to tell me? That I was trying too hard. Even though I denied it, I thought I could not be happy without a partner, so I ignored my intuition and turned every man I met into my new perfect soulmate. Doubts I had, I ignored. I was not impartial at all. I was set on ending my single life, no matter what. Thankfully the universe decided it was time for me to learn this special lesson.

What inside of me attracted the situation? The dogma, that I was not strong enough to handle life by myself. Wanting someone by my side to support me, even if it meant not being myself, attracted men that were not being themselves either. They were looking for fun, casual dating and yes, some were leading me on a little bit. They had to for me to finally snap out of it and realize who I am and what I want.

Which topic was being dealt with? I had to be true to myself, listen to my gut feeling and most of all, I had to learn to take responsibility for my own happiness. Depending on a partner to make my life easy and happy is not fair to him, and frankly impossible to do.

At one point I had finally understood. It took me three years to do so. The man that eventually came into my life is someone I would have never imagined in a million years. Our mind, as beautiful as it may be, does not know what is best for us because it is influenced by to many other things. Only our soul knows. Once I stopped searching for that one, specific type of career oriented, strong man the universe was able to send me the one perfect for me. I don't need him to make me happy, but I love having him in my life.

Another lesson I had to figure out was when my ex-husband decided to sue me for sole custody. He was incredibly hard on me in his statements for court, and the result of the entire torturous process was a change of the visiting regulations for our three children. One child stayed with me; one child decided to go back and forth on a weekly basis; and the third and youngest child decided to move to his father. This broke my heart; however, he suffered the most from all of this fighting that I could not bear to stand in the way of his wish. We all needed peace.

What was the universe trying to tell me? Everything happens for a reason, and if I love my child, I let it go. Everything else would make it worse. I had to have faith, that this is how it is supposed to be and everything will be all right in the end.

What inside of me attracted the situation? Me wanting to control everything and believing I know what is best for everyone. Also the belief that the decision of my child to live with his father automatically makes me a bad mother. And I'm sure not always having the most positive thoughts about my ex-husband played its part in this as well.

Which topic was being dealt with? Letting go and having faith. My intuition told me that letting him go was the only chance he had of finding peace. It was one of the hardest lessons I learned; however, the little one became much more at ease shortly after everything was settled. Although I do not have as much information about him as I would like, since he visits me on every second weekend, I can tell he's happy. His grades are good, he has friends and hobbies, and with him slowly entering puberty, I sometimes have to admit to myself that it is not so bad the way it is. I do have more time for myself, my path and my calling. There are always two sides to every situation, and I needed to focus on the positive one.

The Principle of Rhythm

The importance of the principle of polarity becomes even clearer when understanding the principle of rhythm, which states that rhythmic movements are a continuous rhythmic part of life. Birth to death, dawn to dusk, happy to sad and happy again, sunshine to rain and so on, rhythmic movements are unavoidable and not only part of our material world but the entire universe except for the source itself. After each and every low, comes an equally intense high, just like a constantly turning ferris wheel.

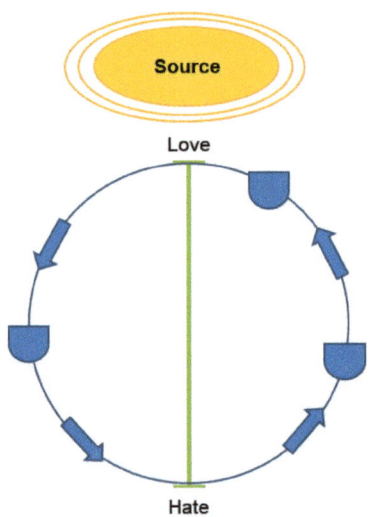

It is up to you how you handle these situations. Just because the little ferris wheel wagon you sit in is going down, does not mean you have to go down with it. We always have the possibility to jump out and stay up. Let the downfall pass you by and neutralize the otherwise most certainly upcoming emotional blues. The goal is to keep your frequency high, being able to handle difficult situations calmly and solution oriented. This can also be trained by, for instance, doing the following:

- Accept what is without judgement
- Realize why it came into your life and answer the three questions mentioned previously
- Keep your focus on the dominant pole
- Take in a meta-position
- Remember that your emotions do not control you

The meta-position makes a constant energy oscillation possible, even if the ferris wheel wagon is going down. That way, you are able to compensate and neutralize a lot of things. In a meta-position you basically visualize yourself being above everything, looking down on your entire life and all your situations in the most objective way possible. You will see, once you manage to keep your energy up, difficult situations will become much clearer and quicker to handle. Life will get easier because you now have the tools to counteract.

ᬽ ● ᬼ

Although I take medication for my depression, I do feel it inside of me every once in a while. I will feel fine for a while then suddenly it will come through again, very much below the threshold, but definitely noticeable. Naturally, this scared me at first. I was afraid the medication would stop working and that things would get back to the way they used to be when I first got ill. I focused on my worries and fears, not noticing how my ferris wheel wagon was taking me down. Once I had realized this, however, I decided to focus on the dominant pole, in this case: trust. Whenever I feel depression inside of me on this subliminal level, I think to myself: "Okay, I suppose it is that time again. I know this will pass within two or three days, and I will be perfectly fine. Until then, I will take it just a little bit slower, spoil myself and concentrate on the beautiful things in my life.

This does not make my depression go away. It is a genetic disorder; it will never go away. But I can handle it. It does not control my life. I accept it and make the best out of the situation. If it wasn't for this disorder, I would have never become the person I am today. I am able to help so many people in similar situations, simply because I have been there, and with unbelievable support from the source and my family, I made it out.

৪০ ● ঞ

For almost all of my life, I was controlled by fear, just as so many people are. I was afraid of not fitting in, of failing, of not being loved, of embarrassing myself and uncountable other things. Well, fear is a deceitful bitch. If you walk through a park, by yourself, in the middle of the night, it is more than okay to be afraid because it is dangerous, and you should not be doing that. However, the fears I am talking about are not real. They are unhealthy thoughts of what MIGHT happen. There is absolutely no guarantee that it WILL happen. Fear and trust are the two opposites of the same emotion. Both are not guaranteed to happen, but trust is so much more pleasant. In addition, trust attracts manifestation as does fear, with the exception that we actually want trust to be manifested. It is the closest to the source. A friend of mine once said: "Do not take your shoes off before reaching the water." In other words, deal with the situation once it is there. Do not worry about it beforehand. There is absolutely no need to take your shoes off and burn your feet in the hot sand if the water is yards away. Fears and worries do not help you. They do not solve your problems, and a lot of the times they are not even real. All they do is slow you down and make you sick.

One book I can highly recommend is "How to stop worrying and start living" from Dale Carnegie. It beholds a very large variety of methods to stop worrying and had an incredible influence on my healing process. One particular method that stuck with me is asking myself the question: What is the worst that can happen? And then accepting it. Having faith in the process and knowing everything will always be all right in the end makes accepting whatever could happen a lot easier. It also dissolves my worries, and in the vast majority of the time, the worst that can happen does not happen. Do not let the deceitful bitch of fear grin and rub her hands in the background, while you worry about everything and anything that could or could not happen. Chose trust instead and deal with the situations as they appear, with the energies of the universe on your side.

The Principle of Cause and Effect

There are no coincidences in life. Everything is due to cause and effect, like a never ending causal chain of events. This network is so complex that most of the time we cannot understand why things are the way they are. Bits and pieces maybe, but never the entire chain of events, because everything is intertwined. We have to trust the process.

So, if coincidences don't exist, is everything predetermined? Why bother making decisions and taking responsibility for your life if you really don't have any say in it?

Because you do have a say in it. In the line of the universal laws, you are able to live a self-determined life. Predetermination and freedom are also two poles on a continuum, whereas freedom is the dominant one. You and everyone else have the choice of either being led by the chain of cause and effect, simply reacting to causes happening to us, or playing the game, being the cause and creating your destiny. In connection to our intuition and in the line of the hermetic principles, we are able to live a self-determined and fulfilling life, in harmony with our divine core. Or we can come to terms with whatever is left over.

Take the meta-position and see where you stand. Step out of the ferris wheel wagon, get your shit together and take charge of your life, for you and every soul in this universe deserves to be happy and loved unconditionally.

„● ‟

For the longest time, I did not spend a lot of thoughts on my own life and how I want to live it. The decision of not making a decision led to me living a life that was not meant for me. Now I could go blaming everyone else for influencing me without truly knowing what is best for me, as if poor little me had no choice in any of it. Well, the truth is, I did have a choice. I chose to not get good grades even though I could have. I chose to not think about what I want to do and had my parents make the decisions for me. Naturally, they decided what they thought would be in my best interest. They did pretty well, but only I am able to reach out to my divine core. No one else is, because no one else is responsible for it. So, when I finally realized this (better late than never), I decided to become a player of my life. I decided to find out what I really want and go after it. It turned out that I love to help others by coaching them, which is why I started the coaching company "Takoda Village". My divine core also loves animals, especially horses. I chose to take in our two ponies because my intuition told me it was the right decision. I was not afraid, and I know I will always be able to take care of them, because they are meant to be in my life for a certain amount of time. When it is time for them to go, it will be painful but all right because I have learned to let go, and I know all of us will be going home to the source eventually. Nothing is ever really dead nor lost forever.

The Principle of Gender

Male and female energy is contained within each living creature. They are basic materials of existence and they depend upon each other. These two energies make creation on all planes possible, materialistically, intellectually and spiritually.

The male energy is responsible for the impulse that is necessary to get started. It delivers the idea, a creative spark, or the cause, if you will.

The female energy is responsible for the necessary implementation. She is more of a back office worker, as she receives the male impulse and gets to work.

A good example is always the creation of life. The male sends, as the female receives and creates. The male energy within you has the ideas and plans, but the female energy within you actually knows how to realize these ideas and plans and does so. It is desirable to have a balance between the male and female energy; this enables you to be even more self-dependent, for you are able to create in and outside of the mind. People with a higher amount of male energy might have plenty of ideas but do not know how to bring them to life. Whereas a person with a very high amount of female energy can bring anything to life, yet lacks the ideas to do so.

Therefore, no matter if you in person are male or female, you contain both male and female energies, and the more in balance they are, the more you can create the life you are meant to live. In case you feel like your energies are not in balance, please do not worry. Once your life returns to balance and fulfillment, your energies will adapt automatically.

The gender principle also helps to understand why some things take longer than we want them to. Inner processes you have started just will not get finished, even though you had the necessary enlightenment weeks ago? Be patient. The female energy is handling it. Be patient with yourself and others, and again, simply trust the process.

߂Ɔ ● Ɔ߃

When I was younger my amount of female energy was much higher than my amount of male energy. I was able to get things done; however, I lacked the ability to see all the possibilities and options to improve my life. The further I walked upon my path, the more aware I became, and the more I healed, the more inner balance I received. Hence the balance between my male and female energies, making it possible for me to create the life I want to have without very much outside help. If I do need help, I know whom to ask or how to research it. Balanced energies lead to a great amount of independence. Furthermore, now that I don't need very much help in my life, I receive it all the time, for the principles of correspondence and vibration make sure to give to me what I am sending. Just because you are able to do a lot of things by yourself does not mean you have to, and helping each other out is one of the greatest things in life.

Universal Assistance

Intro

The seven universal laws are a good and necessary basis to live a healthy and happy life. However, most of us screwed up more than we like to admit; we have lost touch with ourselves; we do not listen to our intuition; we have bad habits and worse dogmas, which we never question. We sell ourselves short because we have forgotten our own worth and sometimes do anything to be loved and sheltered, except love and shelter ourselves. We have forgotten how to live life. We have forgotten this generations ago, which is why many of us cannot realize that what we are feeling is not real happiness, but a substitution and lots of sugarcoating. Often it is what modern civilization makes us believe we want and need and how life should be, but it is not what we are and most definitely not why we are here.

So why are we here? Picture this: You are a beautiful ball of pure energy within the one source of energy. You are completely content. Why leave this perfect place of unconditional love? Because on earth you have the chance to experience touch, laughter, excitement, beauty of all kinds and unforgettable adventures. On earth, you can see your own, wonderful light shine. We only have to stay true to our divine core. This is where it usually goes wrong. We get distracted; we deny what our soul needs to be happy and healthy because we forgot how to listen to it. Before we know it, this magical and beautiful life turns into a harsh and difficult one where everything seems to be one endless battle. It's tiresome and frustrating, and the more we think about it, the farther we go down with it. Some of us end up in extremely dark places, just as I did. However, I am grateful for it, because the only way out was up, and the only way up was by understanding my lessons and solving them.

We all like a good challenge, right? Well, even if you don't, the more you have gotten of your true path, the more challenges you will encounter. The universe will give them to you whether you like it or not, because the source wants you to be happy. Even if you have lost touch with your soul, the source has not, and it cannot bear to see you walk into a direction not meant for you. I often wished for a simple email, explaining to me that what I am doing does not coincide with what my divine core would like me to do. However, it doesn't work this way. For humans to truly understand, they have to experience. They have to have that certain A-HA-effect, in order to internalize the insight. Do you understand why a simple email just will not do?

Almost every difficult or unpleasant situation in life is a universal lesson. You can try to ignore them, as I have done many times for many years, but they will always return in one way or another, and they will not get easier. However, facing them and solving them means conquering your life and growing spiritually. Everything will come to you when the time is right; be patient and take one challenge at a time, and you will see your inner light start to shine again.

It is necessary to reprocess everything that did or does not coincide with the path of your soul. To do this, you may have to remove harming dogmas, heal your inner child, do shadow work, understand how your ego works and most of all, recognize your own worth. I will explain these methods further in the upcoming chapters. Maybe there are a whole lot of obstacles in front of you, but giving in to them will not make your life easier. Once you begin working on yourself, you start a process that is similar to a rolling stone, taking one construction site at a time until you reach your point of origin. Here you recognize how wonderful, unique and valuable you are. You will no longer feel the need to ponder about your past or judge your and others' imperfections. You simply want to enjoy the moment you are in right here and right now. Before you know it, your life will skyrocket, even though there is, of course, always more we can learn.

So why are we here? To live and experience the wonders of life. To fill our soul with magical experiences that make us smile from the inside out. Do not hesitate. The sooner you start, the sooner you can harvest the fulfillment, the love and the happiness you have been entitled to since birth.

Shadows and Mirrors

Shadows are parts of you, which you do not accept or recognize. It could be that they are certain character traits you don't like or maybe even character traits you wish you had but don't believe you do for lack of self-worth. Shadows are easy to spot because they make themselves noticeable through very intense emotions. In most cases, the shadows are on such a subconscious level from suppression, that we are not aware of their existence. We hide them deep within us, which is why we call them shadows.

Has it happened to you, that you find a certain characteristic or habit of someone so annoying you can hardly get over it? Just a little thing, nothing other people would lose a thought about, but it just drives you insane? Congratulations, here we have a perfect shadow. The person is simply reflecting a characteristic you have inside you but refuse to accept. However, unconditional love does not deny any part of you, and if you want to grow spiritually and live the fulfilling life you deserve, it is of the essence to accept and love everything about yourself. As easy it may be to recognize the shadows, it is equally important to set them free. There are some truths we don't want to hear, but that does not make them less true. In fact, for as long as the shadow is hidden deep within you, it is not controllable. It will only grow and get stronger, no matter how much in denial you are. Yet, if you accept every characteristic you have, and bring it into the light, it will become a loved and accepted part of you, and it will be manageable.

Visualization is one way of releasing shadows. However, maybe this method is not right for you. Maybe you need to write down words or simply think about the shadow. A friend of mine, for instance, has to simply become aware of it, and it will basically release itself. Affirmations are also helpful for many people. It is okay to try different methods or invent completely new ones until you find the one that works for you.

As I mentioned before, shadows do not always have to be negative characteristics. For instance, maybe you admire someone in a way you usually don't admire people because this person has characteristics you so wish you had as well. Look inside you. Maybe this is a shadow as well. If it is, set it free. Develop your full potential in every aspect.

The goal is a shadow free divine core, spreading its light in all directions.

ᏸ ● ☌

I always believed I was a very submissive and sweet person. I did not want to be dominant, because growing up with a very dominant father was not always easy. In addition, it made me believe men are supposed to be authoritarian and dominant, not women. I did not want to take charge or lead or manage anything. I was content with being told what was good and right, and I did not like women who acted like I believed men should when it came to dominance and authority. Talk about an unhealthy and totally messed up dogma.

After I had left my husband, I was a single mom of three young boys for about three years. These years where filled with challenges and lessons: some I failed, many I passed and all and all they made me much, much stronger. Yet I still felt like I needed a strong man on my side to take care of my sons and me. It made me look for successful men in high positions, but thankfully, it never worked out. Then, one fine day in April, I met a man who made me happy in many ways. The only thing he lacked was dominance, which at first I could not handle at all until I realized my being annoyed with his kindness was a shadow, combined with a harmful dogma, deep within me. I thought about this for a while, before releasing the shadow. Why should a woman not be strong and manage? Why should she not take charge of the family and organize? The man is not less of a man if he does not feel the need to control everything. After all, we are a team, we live and work at eye level and that is a good thing.

In order to release the shadow, I imagined myself being the dominant characteristic, sitting in a dark corner of a basement. I always release my shadows this way because I am a very visual person. The dominant me was cowered in the corner, yet still proud and strong and covered in ash. I then approached the shadow me with open arms, and when she stood up, I cleaned her up a little bit and hugged her. I whispered in her ear that she is part of me, and I love her just the way she is. She smiled, and we became one.

Now just because I accept and love my dominant side does not mean I have to boss everyone around all the time. On the contrary. However, I realize my own strength, and I am not afraid to take charge if I have to. Also, I am responsible for three children. I am no longer afraid of this responsibility, and I certainly don't need a man or anyone to tell me how I should live my life and raise my boys. I do like having a partner at eye level that I can talk to at any time about anything, whether I need to or not.

Another shadow of mine was Cinderella. How I hated that princess who let herself get pushed around and yelled at and used and abused. She never defended herself; how pathetic. Then again, how weird was it, that a Disney princess who is full of love and kindness could annoy me in such an intense way? I really did not want to see it, but there was no other explanation. Again, I imagined little Cinderella-me, cold and alone in that dark and ashy corner of that basement within. I hugged my little princess and accepted the part of me that never defended and protected myself. I love and forgive my little Cinderella because she is a part of me, and she did her best and deserves love just as everything does.

How does this help me now? I have a dominant and well-fortified side; however, I also have a part of me that can hold back because not every fight is worth the energy. Choose your battles, especially since finding a mutual agreement is usually the better way – the way of love.

The Inner Child

One wonderful thing about small children is their ability to live in the moment. They do not think about what happened five minutes ago and they do not think about what will be either. Toddlers are always in the now, soaking up everything they see and turning this world into a magical place of new adventures. All they care about is joy. Joy in cuddling, joy in playing, joy in eating and so on. They are in touch with their divine core, therefore following their intuition. Everything is an adventure, even if it is the discovery of a wonderful, bright and smooth orange for the very first time. Children see the beauty that many of us take for granted, because when they come onto this earth, they are at their point of origin, ready to experience whatever the soul wishes to.

Unfortunately, life is not always a playground and as we grow up, we experience a variety of situations that a grown up might be able to understand and deal with but a child is not. We hurt ourselves; people disappoint us; or we live through dramatic situations and fear. Children often cannot understand what is going on and start developing strategies to get through certain situations. Strategies many of us still depend upon when we are grown up, not realizing we do not need to do so anymore. Just think about how many people do not like to commit, make decisions and are deeply afraid of making mistakes. Of course, not all of these things always connect to a hurting inner child but, it certainly is worth checking it out, because if it does have something to do with it, it is correctable.

Unhealed inner children create shadows, are often responsible for addictions, fear loss and suffer from jealousy. They cause childish reactions during specific situations like running away from problems, wanting love from someone at any cost or getting defensive very quickly. Hurtful behavior a child has to endure often continues within the following generations, because lacking the knowledge of other ways, the child later passes it on.

Healing your inner child is a major part of healing your life. Healing, however, always contains the following aspects:

- Acceptance of what happened
- Forgiveness for yourself and others
- The capability of letting go
- A promise to yourself for protection and love

First, you need to find out how your child is doing. This may take a little practice, but eventually you will be able to get in touch with it in a matter of seconds. Checking on your inner child is a meditation. Again, you might be someone who visualizes like me, or you simply see words, colors, or something completely different. This you will have to find out for yourself.

⁊ ● ⁋

When I think about my inner child, I see it playing on a gigantic pasture. A beautiful brown cow is usually nearby. However, when I first contacted it, she was cold, lonely and afraid, but mostly she was angry. Thankfully, the book "Das Geheimnis des Herzmagneten" by Ruediger Schache inspired me to do the following meditation:

I put myself in the position of my inner child. I was a young girl of about seven or eight years of age. I was extremely angry because of all the unresolved situations I had to go through. I visualized both of my parents standing right in front of me, in order to tell them all the things that had hurt me. The task was not to get back at them, upset them or make them feel guilty. The task was for my inner child to understand that it is okay to be angry about certain things and to retroactively defend ourselves, even though we know that everything was just the way it was supposed to be, and no one intentionally hurt anyone. I can be angry at something without blame. I can understand a situation and still not like it. All these things are all right. Having my parents in front of me, I began yelling: "I know you did what you could, but it wasn't right that I always felt left alone, that you treated me unfairly, and that I was always afraid in my own home. A child's home should be a shelter, where it is protected and loved. Every child has a naturally given right to shelter and unconditional love. It wasn't right, that….." I yelled at them for quite some time, everything just flew out of me as if it had been waiting to finally be set free. As I spoke my mind, my heart started feeling lighter. Then something wonderful happened. I grew up and turned into the woman I am today, yet I was a better me. A stronger me. I realized I don't need anybody to shelter and love me anymore, because I can and must shelter and love myself.

I turned around and there she was again, my inner child. My parents on the other hand had disappeared, for they had done their deed in this meditation. The child looked at me with big, *wondering eyes. I took her into my arms, held her tight and whispered: "I am so sorry that I was not able to protect you and help you understand. I promise, from now on and forever, to love you unconditionally and protect you from all harm."*

જી ● ß

It is important to mention that many things children go through as a child are not necessarily bad things. The child simply did not understand what was going on. You may have children of your own today. Talk to them, they understand more than we give them credit for, as long as we are honest and include them into our decision making process. Help them understand how the world works and that some choices you make, have to be made, even if it is a somehow hurtful or difficult one.

Ever since the meditation mentioned above, my inner child has been happy. I check on her regularly. Of course, I know that children often can't protect themselves, so why did I apologize? Because guilt is not a rational thing, and it was my way of forgiving everything and letting go. Your child needs to be loved and protected, and it needs to know that it is okay to get angry at situations, even if you, as the grown up, can now understand why things happened the way they did. Emotions are neutral and value-free. You feel them, acknowledge them and let them go. How you react to them may be questionable, but it is always all right to feel them and to speak about them. Otherwise, a new shadow and other obstacles in life are pre-programmed.

Please do not hesitate to check on your inner child and help it, if necessary. Try different measures to do so and find out whichever works best for you. Also, if you feel the need to cry, do so. Crying can be healthy and helps to let go of everything that is no longer needed.

Your Ego – Your Friend

Most of the time, the ego is portrayed as a bad thing. However, this is not the case. It all depends on how your ego is imprinted and how you use it. If you are able to live an aware life in unison with your soul, your ego will be your ally.

Your soul and your ego equate to your earthly personality. The way you look, your preferences, your dislikes and everything that makes you human. Your soul defines you, and your ego is your engine. It is the assistant, the protector, the chauffeur - simply anything your divine core needs to fulfil its dream of a wonderful life.

Without the connection to your soul; however, the ego will still act as an engine, but it will most surely drive in the wrong direction. If you do not listen to your gut feeling, your intuition, many external aspects (media, neighbors, family – everyone and everything who may not want your best or who may not know what is best for you), will influence you. Empower your divine core, not your ego. Only your soul knows what is right for you.

Obviously, the first requirement to a healthy relationship with your ego is feeling your intuition. As this is extremely important, the issue of the gut feeling is a separate, upcoming chapter.

Even if you are connected to your soul and have a good feeling about what is good for you and what is not, there most likely will always be situations in which it is difficult to differentiate. Sometimes I am just not sure whether I want something out of ego reasons or because it truly is what my soul wants or needs. It makes no difference if this concerns a material thing, or something I think about saying or doing. The ego and the soul manage all areas of our life. Therefore, when I get into these situations I ask myself the following questions:

- Do I really need to say, do or have this?
- Why do I want to say, do or have this?
- How do I feel imagining saying, doing or having this?
- Is it necessary, kind and honest to say or do or have?
- If I were love, would I still want to say, do or have this?

This may help filter the soul decisions from the non-soul decisions and you will find that pure ego decisions soon lose value once you realize they are not what is truly good and right for you.

I once was very close to a person who had been practicing Reiki for many years. She is very good at it, therefore able to help many people in need of balance and healing energy. I admire her for that, and when I first got know what she does and what Reiki is all about, I truly believed that this was what I wanted as well.

My friend, who already reached the status of Reiki master, sanctified me, and I started doing my daily exercises, ignoring that I was not feeling good about it at all. In fact, I felt worse with every day until I reached the point of giving up. When I do something that collides with what my soul wants, my soul will give me hints by making me feel a little less happy. This feeling will grow for as long as I keep ignoring my inner divinity. It will grow until it reaches a full depression episode, forcing me to stop whatever I am doing. I wanted to be a Reiki healer so badly that I ignored everything I felt. However, as soon as I gave in and stopped following that particular goal, I started feeling a little bit better, and I realized I wanted to do Reiki for the wrong reasons. I thought with Reiki I would be special and people would admire me for it, just as they admired her. Reiki is a little bit mysterious and unique; it is powerful, and I wanted to be a part of it for those reasons. I did and do want to help people, but Reiki is not my way of doing it.

We often want what we desire in others, but we have to ask ourselves if that would truly make us happy. I am special and unique with or without Reiki. I am able to do a lot of good in this world by listening and counseling. People that have found their own personal happy, no matter what it is, spread a very positive energy which helps change the world. Even if it is the passion for selling luxurious cars to incredibly rich people, for example. Happy is happy. Not all of us have to be therapists, doctors or saints. All we have to do is find our true passion and live it.

The Gut Feeling

All of us have it; however, most of us do not understand or even hear it. Your gut feeling, alias intuition.

This is tragic. Our intuition is our direct connection to our soul and consequently the divine source. Your intuition is your own personal directory and key to a happy and fulfilled life.

As the name implies, your gut feeling is a feeling. If you have lost touch with yourself, it may be a very tiny, suppressed feeling, but I am sure it is there. The more you practice listening to it, the more intense it will get. Eventually you might even feel as if something is whispering to you inside your mind. However, to get to this point may take a little time.

So how do you know if your gut is trying to tell you something?

If your gut feeling is negative, you may experience nausea, doubt, insecurity or fear. You might just get into a rather bad mood or you might even get aggressive. If you do not feel good, especially on an emotional level, then something is going on in your life of which your soul is not approving. If you notice some of these or other symptoms (they may even be of a physical sort like a stiff shoulder) reflect what is going on in your life and how it makes you feel. Have there been changes at home or at work? Have you recently made a bigger decision? Are you thinking about making a bigger decision? Have you gotten into arguments or do you have trouble with any other people? Remember to be honest with yourself. Your intuition will lead you where you need to be, if you let it happen.

If your gut feeling is positive, you will feel happy, blessed and grateful. You will know that whatever is going on is just right without having to justify it. Simply thinking about the situation or the decision will make you smile.

೮つ ● ೮੪

As a child, I took horseback riding lessons. I have always loved horses, but somehow, when puberty hit and we moved into another country on top of that, I stopped. Years went by, I graduated, moved again, started working and eventually got married and had my three amazing boys. At this point, I had lost touch with many things I used to love as a child. My burnout hit, my marriage was over and I started a new job, sharing the office with a woman who owned a horse. We shared that office for about three years;

she is a very sweet person, yet needed a good amount of coaching, and therefore became my first client as well as a good friend.

One day, I don't even remember how we got on the subject, I mentioned that I would like to sit on a horse again, since it has been so many years. "Well that's easy!" she said. "Who do you know who owns a horse and is sitting right in front of you?" Only a few days later I visited her and her horse, Bennie, at the stable. I cleaned him, got to know him, and then got to ride him. My friend took another horse. It was late summer, the sun was shining and a light breeze was blowing. As we slowly rode through the fields, I had the incredible feeling of time and space standing still. I had never before been more in the moment, at least not during my grown-up years. I cherished every second of the time with Bennie and the absolute worry-free and content feeling he gave me. I knew this was my gut saying: Do you see? Horses make you happy, Judy. Follow that dream and the source will support you. I did, and now I have two horses of my own. They live on a pasture that we are allowed to use free of charge, under the condition that we take good care of it. I did not pay much for the horses either, because the owners' priority was to find a good home for them and all of this happened within the short span of two years.

My gut feeling is very distinct when it comes to warning me as well. During my time as a single mom, I met a very nice man. He lived approximately 200 miles away. We talked every night for hours, shared many of the same opinions, talked about all kinds of different issues and had a great time. Both of us wanted a serious relationship, and we were sure to be perfect for each other. Very spontaneously, he decided to visit me. I was so excited and happy and could not wait for him to arrive. When he finally did, I opened the door and for a fraction of a second, I heard a loud and clear NO inside my head. Now that was not part of the plan, so I pushed it away by reminding myself of how many nice and fun conversations we had and how everything else seemed to be perfect as well.

My gut feeling, however, was set on coming out on top. Looking back, it was as if it was saying: "You will learn your lesson tonight and you will hear me, no matter what it takes!" Therefore, as we got closer, I started feeling sicker. I wanted to fall in love with him. I really did. In addition, I did not want to send him home with a rejection, after he had just driven

200 miles in a cloak-and-dagger operation. I wanted to at least give it a try. Forcing myself resulted in me feeling extremely nauseous, lying outside on the terrace, suffering from a very heavy depressive episode. Fortunately, he was sensitive enough to realize that my feeling ill had something to do with him, and decided to drive back home in the middle of the night. I cried and apologized; however, I was very relieved as well. As soon as he had driven away, I started feeling better. That night it became crystal clear to me how my intuition speaks to me and how my inner watchdog takes care of me. It was a very hard and very important lesson for which I am very grateful. He and I are still friends today.

⁎ ● ⁎

Life itself is not a war. You do not have to keep on fighting. If you follow you true path, gentle strokes of fate will guide you, if you let them.

Remember, every single human being is different. Everyone has different dreams, wishes, needs and desires. While your one neighbor might feel fulfillment with eleven sports cars in his garage, your other neighbor might feel it walking barefoot through a park, feeding birds and hugging trees. Do not worry about other people's fulfillment; find your own and live the life you deserve.

If necessary, protect and defend yourself. Your intuition is of great assistance here. It will let you know if your soul is in danger or even if you simply step outside of your path. Your highly trained watchdog always lets you know if something is good or not. Train it, listen to it and lead the life your soul is meant to live. Make the most out of it. Always reflect the energies you are sending out. Are they loving or hurtful? Do your actions make you happy or are they stressful? We will always encounter situations we do not really like but have to go through. We are spiritual beings; however, we live in a very materialistic world, so it is important to find a way of combining the two with the help of your mind and intuition, building a bridge to combine all the energetic planes.

Dogmas

Every person has personal dogmas. A dogma is an opinion or a firm belief that you do not question. Although this in itself is not a bad thing at all, for we all have our system of beliefs, often we are influenced by dogmas we don't even know we have. Dogmas we took on while growing up because of the things we were taught or the examples we were given. I have talked about one of my dogmas before, thinking the man has to be the one in charge, making the decisions and taking care of everything, while the woman supports him. No one has ever told me this is the way it is supposed to be, I simply had the impression as a child, watching my parents as well as being easily intimidated by authoritative personalities. This dogma was wrong for me, but I never questioned it until life's lessons forced me to.

In order to find your true happiness, it is important to find and sort through your dogmas to get rid of the ones holding you back. This is best done by questioning yourself. Whenever you think you cannot do or say or even think something, ask yourself "why?" If it is a good dogma, you will have a reasonable answer. However, if it isn't, you will most likely have no convincing reason. "Because that is just the way it is" will not do in most cases. "All of my friends are doing it this way" does not count either. Your friends' happiness is not your happiness. Another answer may be "What will others think?" It does not matter what others will think because people think what they want to think. As long as you are worried about other people's opinions, you can never be truly free.

Remember you are here to live a fulfilling life. Even if it means doing something nobody else would classify as fulfilling. For example, if you decide to work part time, knowing you will still have enough money to live a normal life, but more time to find and live your true passion, why not do it? You're not hurting anyone. It is okay to work part time, even if your children are grown and even if you don't have any at all. There is no job-police telling you, you cannot do that. Just because it has never been this way or it is nonstandard, does not mean it should not be this way. Of course, this is just one example of many. Question your reasoning behind your choices and find the dogmas blocking you, one after another. It will set you free, widen your path and may even open doors for you that you never would have thought were an option at all.

ꕤ●ꕤ

Besides the major dogma I mentioned before, believing that women should not be the ones in charge, I will mention a dogma of another kind which is hardly as serious, yet still important.

As my best friend, Ulli, got married for the second time, she and her husband decided to celebrate a very casual and fun outdoor wedding party that included spending the night in tents. Since it was such a casual occasion, she bought herself an outfit, which was quite cute, yet far from the typical white wedding dress most women love to wear on their special day. She went with a nice pair of jeans and a cute black blouse with white polka dots. When her mom heard of the outfit she said: "What? A black blouse? You can't wear black on your wedding?" Ulli looked at her and replied: "Why not? Is there a wedding police that will come and arrest me for wearing the wrong color?" And that was that.

This is a perfect example of little dogmas many of us have and never question. Not all of them have to be intense and deeply mind changing, but getting rid of each harmful one, no matter how insignificant it may seem, will make your life a little happier.

Self-Worth

Self-worth seems to be the root of it all. In all the cases I have met, the root of their problems was not knowing how much they are worth. A healthy and accurate self-worth will make you protect and love yourself. If you truly realize what you are, namely a part of the divine source, and that you are incredibly valuable, as is every living soul, you will make sure to set your own boundaries, stand up for yourself and your beliefs, attracting people into your life that will do the same, because that is the principle of correspondence.

Imagine your life being a beautifully wrapped present, given to you by the source. You do not realize its worth and therefore, do not treat it very well. Your present lies in some corner of your home, the wrapping paper is crinkled and the package has dents in it. The people entering your life see the present and what do you think they will believe? That it is the most valuable thing they have ever seen? No! They see a damaged box lying in the corner that obviously is not worth very much. Most likely, they will kick it out of the way to make room for themselves. Not because these people are necessarily bad, but simply because no one realizes that they are actually mistreating something precious.

What do you think will happen if you treat your present as if it is the most valuable thing you have ever possessed? You cherish and polish it; you protect it and make sure nothing bad will happen to it. You put the present in a special place where you can watch over it, adore it and make sure everyone else can as well. No one would dare to mistreat it because it is obvious how important and precious the present is. People entering your life will realize this and give it the careful and loving treatment your life deserves.

ࡣ ● ߣ

For whatever reasons, I did not realize my own worth for a very long time. I never put myself first; when it came to giving in for the sake of peace, I would do so. I would do anything to prove to everyone that I am a kind and lovable person people could be grateful to know. I was not proving anything to anyone, least of all to myself. Trying to make everyone happy not only led to me getting ill, it sent energies into the world that told others it was all right to treat me like I was beneath them. As if my feelings did not matter as much. For as long as I put myself last in line, others would do the same. That is how life works.

The more I developed, the more awareness of my own worth I received. Eventually I stopped living up to other people's expectations, because I had created my own. It is my goal to reach my own benchmark and I do not put myself last in line in order to please everyone else first. In fact, I try to avoid lines in general. I do what I can for the people I love, including myself. These are the energies I am sending out, therefore receiving corresponding energies. I do not allow others to mistreat me, and I meet less and less people that feel like they have to. If someone does treat me in a way that is upsetting, I usually react instantly and automatically. In many cases, the treatment has nothing to do with life teaching me a lesson anymore, but rather with life trying to teach the other person a lesson. Sometimes we are simply figures filling out a role of some sort. However, your intuition will tell you that as well.

Looking back, I am very grateful for everyone helping me in this way, for it lead to rediscovering myself and my purpose in life.

৪ে ● ৫ব

As I have mentioned before, every soul is precious and of priceless worth. However, not every person is a good person. We do not know what people had to endure and how they became whatever they are. Sometimes the soul is buried deep within, and although it still is a priceless thing, the person itself has lost touch with it and does not act according to its needs. It is okay to stay away from people that are not good for you. You do not have to endure bad treatment or negativity of any sort because you believe the divine core of everyone forces you to. It is enough to love the divine core within everyone, including your own.

Energy

Everything is always about energy, for energy is what we are. Energy is our fuel, and the source is our gas station. As long as we are connected to our divine core and as long as we manage to heal ourselves, know our worth and follow our goals and dreams, we will not run out of fuel. However, what happens if we lose the connection?

Well, we have to find another way to gas up. Without the connection to the source, the only place left to get the energy we need is taking the energy of other people. This is not a conscious process. The book "The Celestine Prophecy" from James Redfield has a great description of how unconnected people receive their energies. He describes four different types of people: the intimidator, the interrogator, the aloof and the poor me. For convenience reasons, I refer to the different types as "he" in my description below. This is not meant to offend anybody; it simply makes the flow of reading easier. All "unconnected" people, male or female, will correspond to one or more of these types.

The intimidator is usually very loud and dominant. Many people feel insecure or even afraid in his or her presence, which makes the intimidator feel powerful, therefore receiving energy.

The interrogator is a genius when it comes to asking questions. He will ask so many different questions until given an answer he does not agree with. Then he will start criticizing the interrogated person, again making them feel inferior and insecure.

The aloof is a very mysterious person. He will not reveal very much about himself, in order for people to be curious and fascinated by him. This is a more passive way of receiving energy.

The poor me is a person who feels very sorry for himself. Bad things always seem to happen to him. He feeds upon other people's sympathy. A poor me will not be open for solutions. Give him a solution for a problem and he will no longer be able to use the problem as an energy source. Therefore, he usually has plenty of excuses for every solution option you deliver.

What kind of person are you? I used to be a mix of the aloof and the poor me in my first stages. When I started to develop spiritually, I turned into a mix of the aloof and the intimidator. Thankfully, now I am connected, so usually I am no longer in need of other people's energies. I usually have a permanent line to the source. If I fall back into old habits, sucking energy off of others, I usually realize this quickly, because the taken energy does not feel as good. It is as if it leaves a bad taste in my mouth because it was not mine to take.

So how do you deal with energy thieves? It is important to remember that they do not mean to steal your energy. They have no other option at the time.

If you know how much you are worth, you know that no one has the right to mistreat you. Yelling and scaring people is not a respectful way to treat others, therefore you should not care who it is yelling, that is yelling at you. Treat them with respect, demand the same and it will become hard to intimidate you.

You are a human and you make mistakes. It's perfectly normal. So, if someone happens to find one you made, then answer for it. People may criticize your decisions in a respectful manner as well. If you are convinced of the decision, stand for it, no matter what others think. You are a capable person. Try to reflect your own opinions and decisions on a regular basis. Be open for discussions, and if others have convincing arguments, you may change your mind. However, criticizing for the sake of criticizing is a waste of time and energy and does not need to be tolerated by you.

Aloof people should not raise your interest. If a person wants to open up to you welcome them and be interested in what they have to say. If they don't, that's fine, too. Do not chase after anyone, begging to let you in. Why? Because you do not need to do so. You probably have friends and family, and you definitely have yourself. There is no need to fight for other people's attention. No one should.

Poor me people are a bit tricky. You have to find out how far along they are. Is it a poor me person or is it someone truly searching for help? Clarity usually comes with the offering of solutions. Poor me people have a "yes, but" excuse for everything, and you will soon realize that they do not want a solution; they want your sympathy, therefore your energy. Once you realize this, you might not be able to sympathize any longer. I am always sorry for people who have not found their way of connecting to the universal energy yet, but feeding their energy needs will not help them in their process to do so. Save your energy for the people who are ready for it.

This may sound a little arrogant, but it really is not. It's healthy. You are protecting your own energy level. You can give energy to people all the time; however, give it freely to those who are on their path, finding their way, wanting to understand and grow. Do not let it be taken involuntarily, for that will not only be exhausting for you, it oversteps your personal boundaries and reduces your frequency of energy.

Your Own Personal Circle of Protection

You cannot change people and you should not try, for no one has the right to. You can only change yourself. Everyone goes on their own path and chooses to grow or not to grow at their own pace. People will always be what they are. If a person desires my support, I will gladly give it to them. I will be honored to, because it is a sign of trust toward me, which I am very grateful for. People who do not want to change, whether it is that they are not ready or they do not feel the need to because everything seems to be just fine, should never be forced to. They choose reaction instead of action. They choose to remain in the little wagon of the ferris wheel and not to step out before going down. They choose predestination and that decision should not be judged by anyone. Especially since no one can know what goes on in other people's minds and lives, and none of us ever stop learning. We might believe someone is living the "wrong" life, even if they truly aren't. They may be absolutely happy and fulfilled. Even if they are not, it is not up to you to change that. It is up to them.

To help differentiate when you are supposed to step into other people's lives, you can visualize a circle around yourself. The circle beholds all that concerns you: your life, your family, your friends, your job, your free time and so on. So, if you see things that may not be right, do not immediately get involved unless it is within your circle. It is natural for people to be ungrateful for advice; they did not ask for. It may even be perceived as an imposition. Of course, this does not mean you should look away in serious situations of need or emergencies. Sometimes you have to get involved!

⁝ ● ⁜

A former colleague of mine was a very troubled poor me-person. At first, I felt the need to help her because I was able to relate to her issues and thought I would be able to. She was not ready. She received too much energy from other people's sympathy. Getting involved would have made it worse. If you keep catching people when they fall, they will not learn to take charge and responsibility for their own happiness. Birds do not learn to fly if you do not let them fall first, and people cannot heal if you do not let them fall either. This is very hard to do. You can show them the door to another way of life, but they will have to be the ones walking through it. After I had realized this, I envisioned my circle and decided not to do anything unless she entered it. Should she remain a poor me, I would have to distance myself. Should she be searching for support, ready to change, I would gladly be there for her and I would try to catch her every time. She never entered my circle and that is fine too. I am not the one to help her, and I hope the universe sent her just the person she needed.

ଚଃ ● ଔଓ

If you don't create that imaginary boundary, you end up getting involved in situations for the wrong reasons. Again, I am not talking about emergencies of any kind. It is perfectly all right to offer your support and to let people know you understand and you might be able and glad to help. However, people must voluntarily come to you without feeling pressured. They have to make that decision when they are ready to do so. Chasing after them would be giving your ego too much control. This does not just apply to spiritual growth and healing. It applies to any area of life. There is never a need to impose on anyone, and getting involved in other people's lives without them asking for your opinion or advice or support is just that, an imposition.

Live your life in love, connected to your divine core; be kind and helpful to yourself and others, and the right people will come to you when the time is right. Trust the process, never stop working, have faith in the source and do not believe for one second that all of this applies to everyone but you.

Do you want to live the life meant for you? One of happiness and fulfillment? Then you need to pick yourself up and get your shit together. I mean that in the most loving way possible. You need to take responsibility for your life, stop blaming others, heal yourself and get going. You cannot change what happened, so change the now, for the now is ultimately all you have. Spend it wisely. Every second in which you are hateful, frustrated, envious or sad, is low frequency energy you send and receive. Try to keep those slow emotions at a record low using all of the methods mentioned above.

Every soul has a birthright of unconditional love and fortune. That includes you! Every soul is part of the divine source of the universe and therefore of priceless value. That includes you! Every soul is connected to all the other souls as well as the divine source. That includes you!

Whatever is in us is therefore in everything else as well. Keep your body, mind and soul healthy and balanced; remember that you always reap what you sow, that you do not have to go down into those dark places, even if life gets harder at times, and please remember that you always have a choice. Choose the dominant pole: the energy that feels good and right for you. Depending on where you start off, you might have a difficult path ahead of you. Let the universe and all its wonders support you and show you the way. Detours are sometimes necessary; trust the process and the incredible network of the heavenly source. You have all you need to live the fulfilling life you deserve right inside of you. Always feel loved and special, for that is exactly what you are.

Thank you

Thank you to all my teachers in life for taking different roles to help me understand and learn my lessons. I know I was not always an easy student to teach to.

Thank you mom and dad for not giving up on me, even though my way of life is so different from yours. I know I was not always a pleasant child to have and we did have our difficulties. The more grateful I of the relationship we have today.

Thank you Ulli for walking this path with me, always being there, joining me on this special journey with all your patience and love and understanding. You have seen my darkest places and my lightest ones and have never left my side. You are such a special and wonderful person and I love you very much.

Thank you Kai, Hagen and Erik for choosing me as your mother, you are the most wonderful sons anyone could ever ask for. I am sorry for any difficulties I may have caused. I love you so much and am very proud to be your mom.

Thank you Brian for supporting all of my crazy ideas, for being there through all of my different phases and for loving me for who I am. You are wonderful and kind and I am very grateful to be a part of your life.

Thank you Anne for proofreading this book for me.

Thank you Rich for being an inspiration and a wonderful human being.

Thank you to all the authors that have helped me with their wonderful literature. Some of them I have mentioned in this book, yet there are so many more.

Thank you God for this wonderful life and the love, the energy and the support I know I will always receive from you.